T0125498

ThE PoWER oF WORDS

ThE PoWER OF WORDS

Change Your Vocabulary
Change Your Outlook in Life In 31 Days

ANTHONY M. VANDYKE

NEW YORK

ThE PoWER oF WORDS
Change Your Vocabulary Change Your Outlook in Life In 31 Days

© 2014 Anthony M. VanDyke. All rights reserved.

No part of this publication may be reproduced or transmitted in any form or by any means, mechanical or electronic, including photocopying and recording, or by any information storage and retrieval system, without permission in writing from author or publisher (except by a reviewer, who may quote brief passages and/or show brief video clips in a review).

Disclaimer: The Publisher and the Author make no representations or warranties with respect to the accuracy or completeness of the contents of this work and specifically disclaim all warranties, including without limitation warranties of fitness for a particular purpose. No warranty may be created or extended by sales or promotional materials. The advice and strategies contained herein may not be suitable for every situation. This work is sold with the understanding that the Publisher is not engaged in rendering legal, accounting, or other professional services. If professional assistance is required, the services of a competent professional person should be sought. Neither the Publisher nor the Author shall be liable for damages arising herefrom. The fact that an organization or website is referred to in this work as a citation and/or a potential source of further information does not mean that the Author or the Publisher endorses the information the organization or website may provide or recommendations it may make. Further, readers should be aware that internet websites listed in this work may have changed or disappeared between when this work was written and when it is read.

Unless otherwise stated, all Scripture quotations are taken from the King James Version of the Bible. All rights reserved worldwide.

ISBN 978-1-61448-610-7 paperback
ISBN 978-1-61448-611-4 eBook
ISBN 978-1-61448-612-1 Audio
Library of Congress Control Number: 2013931151

Morgan James Publishing
The Entrepreneurial Publisher
5 Penn Plaza, 23rd Floor,
New York City, New York 10001
(212) 655-5470 office • (516) 908-4496 fax
www.MorganJamesPublishing.com

Edited by PenReady LLC
Cover Design by:
Rachel Lopez
www.r2cdesign.com

Interior Design by:
Bonnie Bushman
bonnie@caboodlegraphics.com

In an effort to support local communities, raise awareness and funds, Morgan James Publishing donates a percentage of all book sales for the life of each book to Habitat for Humanity Peninsula and Greater Williamsburg.

Get involved today, visit
www.MorganJamesBuilds.com.

Habitat for Humanity®
Peninsula and
Greater Williamsburg
Building Partner

To Nicole

This book is dedicated to my devoted wife and best friend, Nicole. Nicole, you have been such an inspiration to me. You have taught and modeled honesty and integrity. I am completing this book as you are starting your first chemotherapy treatment. You are on the other side of the room as I watch the drugs go into your body to help cure the breast cancer that you have been diagnosed with. I am very fortunate to be in love with such a beautiful, kind and considerate woman of God.

TABLE OF CONTENTS

	INTRODUCTION	ix
Day 1:	W.O.R.D.S.	1
Day 2:	O.P.P.O.R.T.U.N.I.T.Y.	4
Day 3:	P.O.W.E.R.	8
Day 4:	D.R.E.A.M.S.	11
Day 5:	P.O.T.E.N.T.I.A.L.	15
Day 6:	N.O.W.	18
Day 7:	E.N.R.I.C.H.	21
Day 8:	F.O.C.U.S.	25
Day 9:	F.E.A.R.	29
Day 10:	V.O.I.C.E.S.	33
Day 11:	F.A.I.L.U.R.E.	36
Day 12:	P.E.A.C.E.	39
Day 13:	**O.V.**E.R.F.L.O.W.	42
Day 14:	O.V.**E.R.**F.L.O.W.	46
Day 15:	O.V.E.R.**F.L.**O.W.	50
Day 16:	O.V.E.R.F.L.**O.W.**	53

Day 17:   **F.R.**U.S.T.R.A.T.I.O.N.   56

Day 18:   F.R.**U.**S.T.R.A.T.I.O.N.   59

Day 19:   F.R.U.**S.T.R.**A.T.I.O.N.   62

Day 20:   F.R.U.S.T.R.**A.**T.I.O.N.   65

Day 21:   F.R.U.S.T.R.A.**T.I.O.N.**   68

Day 22:   **R.I.**S.K.   71

Day 23:   R.I.**S.K.**   74

Day 24:   **R.E.W.**A.R.D.S.   77

Day 25:   R.E.W.**A.R.D.S.**   80

Day 26:   F.A.V.O.R.   83

Day 27:   R.A.C.E.   86

Day 28:   P.A.I.N.   89

Day 29:   W.I.N.N.E.R.S.   92

Day 30:   V.I.C.T.O.R.Y.   95

Day 31:   The Flow of Words   99

          About The Author   103

INTRODUCTION

Without words, communication would almost be impossible. During my journey of life I have found that certain words have served as ointment for my spirit. In the book of John, the first chapter, we find that words were in the beginning before any manifestations had taken place. God spoke a word and life as we know it began to take form and manifestations soon followed. Words still have the same power today. Proverbs 18:21, says that "death and life are in the power of the tongue"; therefore you must learn to train your mouth to speak that which will help make your journey more productive. Often, the words you hear and speak become too common and have little meaning. David said in Psalm 119:11, "thy word I have hid in my heart that I might not sin against thee." Life is too short and you must understand your life journey is directly connected to the words you speak.

This devotional is not a, "name it claim it" book, but a guide that will help you on your life journey as it has helped me to become a better pastor, Christian, husband, father, friend and encourager to many. Each day I will share with you words that have meant so much to me and carry awesome power.

I knew "The Power of Words" had to be written, after I started working with a local radio show, FM 100.9, "Rejoice in the Morning" with Mike Chandler. When I first started on the broadcast, we would choose a different topic each day for discussion with our live audience. I believe our initial topic was about opportunities. God had given me a revelation on what the word opportunity meant and I showed it to the show's host. Shortly thereafter he gave me the chance to share my revelation with his radio audience. I was amazed at the response received from the live audience. At that moment I realized something big had just taken place and I knew God was up to something.

As time progressed the Holy Spirit would reveal deeper meaning of words that people used on a daily basis. The power of words can never be underestimated, they have healing power when used and administered properly. The morning show host suggested putting these words into a book and after much resistance and procrastination *The Power of Words* began to take form.

For best results, find a quiet place to read each lesson for the next 31 days. You are setting the foundation for your future. Remember Prov. 18:21, "death and life are in the power of the tongue." The words you hear the most are the ones articulated from your mouth. Adopt a new vocabulary and transform your life.

Day

1

W.O.R.D.S.

Weapons that
Open up new opportunities which
Release your
Destiny and desires
Suddenly

You must use W.O.R.D.S as a weapon to encourage yourself. W.O.R.D.S administered properly will provide the strength you need to make those dreams come true and they will catapult you into your destiny track.

Consistently throughout this devotional tool you will hear me say "Power of Words can never be underestimated". Each day I hear people complaining about their lives, with little to no effort to reverse their situations. At work the other day there was a group of men complaining about being broke and stating that they all were "poor and will always be that way". My spirit was grieved because I knew that change was possible for them. They held the power to reverse their financial situations starting by declaring God's best for their lives. Little did they know financial breakthrough was possible for them. I wanted to jump and tell them to stop wasting time talking negatively and to do something about their situation.

What those men failed to realize is their own words served as weapons of mass destruction. Wikipedia says weapons are "a tool or instrument used in order to inflict damage or harm to living beings—physical or mental." From that definition I gather my words can inflict damage on my situation or me personally. I choose to inflict damage to the things I am battling rather than on myself. Today as you continue your journey remember only to speak life into your situations and monitor the words you declare. As you continue to monitor your words a new destiny will be unveiled and released in your life. The power of words will carry you to new heights in your life. Do big things today and try something different and you will be amazed at how life turns in your favor.

Worksheet

Day

2

O.P.P.O.R.T.U.N.I.T.Y.

Obstacles you can conquer

Problems you can deal with

Potential failures you can overcome

Open doors if you're willing to walk through the unknown

Reach for the stars understanding you have nothing to lose

Train your mind to think possibilities rather than failures

Understand that nothing happens for a sleeper but dreams

Never take for granted the promises of today

Implement positive change

Travel down the road of the unknown

Yield only to the Spirit of God

Midsummer 2008 was a trying time for the world economy. The stock market crashed in the U.S. and it caused a tail spin in the world economic system. Most Americans did what appeared to be the logical thing, they pulled back spending and put their money in safe predictable vehicles for financial return. Warren Buffet did the exact opposite; he started investing and spending all kinds of money, because he understood what goes down, must eventually rebound.

Well, I stand to tell you the recession is nearly over and billions of dollars were made during the recession. Those that prospered were knowledgeable of economics and in a position to take advantage of the opportunities that presented themselves. Your life journey is full of **opportunities,** but you must be in position to receive all that God has in store for you. Do not live the life of regret, wondering if you should have made the move. Instead, stop talking about it, put a plan of action together and seize your **opportunity**.

Life is too short to discount today, hoping for a better tomorrow. God wants you to take advantage of what has been presented to you at this point in time. No matter what happens you must shake off the dust and be committed to moving forward in life. Success is never by chance; those that achieve greatness in life often times have fought through some kind of adversity. "The Power of Words" will cause you to travel down the road unknown, but you must always know that God will never leave nor forsake you.

As you start your day understand that each situation you face is an O.P.P.O.R.T.U.N.I.T.Y for you to improve your current situation. Speak into the atmosphere what you need and desire and watch your day begin to format what you have declared in the atmosphere. Train your mind to see and speak the possible and you will be amazed at what happens. As a top sales agent each morning I woke up with an expectation to sell at least one car a day. That mentality allowed me to remain a top salesman year after year and month after month. Opportunities are what we make them and how we perceive things. I choose to live life thinking positively and speaking positively about each situation no matter how difficult it may appear to be. Stop procrastinating and complaining and take advantage of the cards you have been dealt. This is your second day to take advantage of the momentum. Know there is power in your words and take advantage of every O.P.P.O.R.T.U.N.I.T.Y that comes your way.

Worksheet

P.O.W.E.R.

Potential to cause pain or happiness harnessed
On the inside waiting to present itself positive or negative
When the proper season presents itself for release
Embracing the danger if not monitored
Real tragedy harm and danger can occur

I have discovered most people fail to realize their P.OW.E.R and true potential in life. Without understanding the P.OW.E.R you have over your situations, you cannot maximize life. Life has a way of delivering blows that you do not expect. If you are not careful, you will find yourself powerless and limited on what you can achieve in life. Living a life without P.OW.E.R can lead you down the path of hopelessness and depression.

I remember back several years ago, going through a period of feeling powerless and depressed. My mortgage brokerage firm closed, leaving me without income and no plan of attack to get that income back. Several months went by and I was forced to take any job that paid any kind of wage. My debts began to pile up and I had no answer of how to provide for my family. Life had flipped on me. I was in turmoil on the inside and I was asking God why he had done this to me. It seemed like months had gone by and I heard nothing from God. I thought he had abandoned me. Things had begun to change for the worst in my life and I felt powerless and worthless.

The turning point to getting P.OW.E.R back was discovering my potential again. I had to recommit to the things that brought the most success to me in life. I realized that God had bestowed the ability upon me to talk and speak kind words to people. I realized the power I had in getting people to trust me. I realized the power I had to help people solve problems. Once I put all those things together, I became successful again. I soon discovered success is not built on how much money we have but the ability to use what God has empowered us to do. Understanding how I was built was the key to getting my power back. Today will you take time out to understand what you are good at and be true to yourself and the power of God will soon show itself in your life again.

Worksheet

Day

4

D.R.E.A.M.S.

Deep
Rooted
Emotional
Anticipations
Manifested in the
Spirit of People

I have discovered that as people get older they stop dreaming and they become more silent about their life goals and personal ambitions. Disappointments and failures have a way of keeping people from stretching out and doing more. The greatest battle that you will face in your journey to improve over the next 31 days is the battle of the mind. Your mental state must remain positive and clutter free in order to keep dreaming and remaining relevant in your approach to life. Those that are not afraid to keep dreaming are the ones who excel in life.

Yes, D.R.E.A.M.S are deep-rooted emotional attachments in the spirit of a person and once they are realized, it gives fuel to the individual to push beyond levels of comfort in order to bring those things to life. We are all born to dream until some adult tells us what we cannot do. Advice must be measured by the content in which it has been given. Before I take advice from anyone, I look at what they have accomplished to make sure they are qualified to give me life changing information.

Several years ago, I started a small mortgage brokerage firm with little to no experience running my own company. It was always a dream of mine to run a business of my own and employ people. I took a chance and ignored all the critics. I discovered all the negative people who warned me of all the potential disadvantages of running a business had never run a business and had no credible reference points for their comments.

I kept true to my dream and believed God for insight on how to make this company work. ABC Mortgage Funding took off in a matter of months. The word spread throughout the community about what I was doing and my phone rang off the hook. My business grew to 13 employees and my income netted six-figure profits within two years of being in business. Dreams are possible when you follow a few simple procedures

- Gather Information on what you plan to do
- Get a model or mentor of what your venture should be
- Get the best educational material you can afford

- Goals must be written down both short and long term
- Get better each day and always look for ways to improve

There are only a few things that separate the contenders from the pretenders. Contenders are intentional in their approach to life. They do not wait for things to happen; they are committed to planning while holding their dreams in the backdrop of their imaginations. My friend, as you travel on your new 30-day journey keep dreaming and believing and remember there is power in words.

Worksheet

Day
5

P.O.T.E.N.T.I.A.L.

Possibility
Of greatness and
Talents that need to be
Elevated and increased into
Nothing less
Than God's
Initial plan for you
Allowing you exposure and
Limits removed in your life

P.O.T.E.N.T.I.A.L is so awesome. It gives you a glimpse into the future of what is possible, provided discipline and hard work becomes part of your life style. I have seen many people with all the P.O.T.E.N.T.I.A.L in the world and no gold at the end of the rainbow. When potential is realized, pain and disappointments are minimal. There are several roadblocks to P.O.T.E.N.T.I.A.L. The greatest is the inability to be consistent in core values. Core values are

- Honesty with yourself
- Honesty with others
- Humble spirit
- Heart to listen to criticism
- Helping hand to others without benefit to yourself

Sam Hurd was a promising football player who had awesome potential and promise. December 2011 he was arrested in Chicago and accused of being a drug king pin. Sam Hurd had enough money because he had just signed a multi-million dollar contract with the Chicago Bears. Sam is representative of many young people today; they refuse to work harder to develop the God-given talents they already have.

P.O.T.E.N.T.I.A.L must be coupled with discipline to go the distance in life and that distance often times requires the individual to exhaust all means at hand to bring that future reality to past. There is nothing wrong with wanting more from life as long as the approach attainment is with hard work and integrity. Be honest and do a self-assessment to make sure you are not wasting time, talent, or resources.

Worksheet

Day
6

N.O.W.

New creative and fresh
Opportunities
Working for you

N.O.W is the time to make changes. I have often discovered that procrastination is the key ingredient to failure. There are so many talented people in the world, yet there are so many people under achieving. If you are like most people, you often are looking for the perfect opportunity to move forward and start pursuing what you always dreamed about doing. My friend can I tell you something? There is never going to be the right time. You must move forward N.O.W. Yesterday is already here and tomorrow is just a few minutes away. I started writing this book three years ago but I just got the courage to finish it.

Something major happened in my life to wake me up. May 2012 my beautiful wife of almost 20 years was diagnosed with breast cancer. I have no worries that we will beat the disease but it woke me up and I made a decree that I would no longer waste time. I also vowed never to let people waste my time. Tomorrow is not promised to any of us and we must redeem the time now. My friend, you have the rest of your life to finish what you started. You have almost completed one week of learning the *Power of Words,* and please remember that you must move N.O.W. God bless and have a great day.

Worksheet

Day

7

E.N.R.I.C.H.

Educate yourself
Never give up on yourself
Remain True to Yourself
Invest in yourself
Capture every opportunity for yourself
Hunger to develop yourself

The greatest investment you will ever make in life is to yourself. We live in a very busy world with little time to relax and evaluate where we are personally. Growing up as a child my father taught me the tricks to growing a good garden year after year. The secret was making sure the soil had plenty of nutrients. Each crop has a way of absorbing the ground of the necessary strength it needs to produce good fruits and vegetables. Therefore, each year we would replenish the ground with fertilizer, manure, and other soil enriching material.

Life is the same way. You must be committed to enriching who you are and education is the primary way to remain relevant. Never stop learning; each day there is something we can learn in order to improve who we are. My pastor, Bishop Rosie O'neal, said to me several years ago, "the difference between me this year and next year are two things: the people I associate with and the books I read." This one piece of advice has made all the difference to me.

Secondly, once you start the education process it is very important that you be committed to not giving up. The scripture says the race is not given to the swift nor to the strong, but he that endureth to the end (Eccl. 9:11).

Finally remaining focused is the key to changing your life in the next 31 days. Focus is the commitment to moving forward while not yielding to distractions and temptations to quit. Take to time to capture every opportunity that presents itself to you. Remember the greatest asset you have is you, therefore commit to developing yourself and you will soon see the world as you know it change before your very eyes. Have a great day and remember you are worth the investment and never stop hungering to improve yourself.

Reflections from Day One to Seven

What word(s) meant the most to you?

_____

_____

_____

_____

_____

_____

_____

_____

_____

_____

_____

How can you apply those words to your life?

_____

_____

_____

_____

_____

_____

_____

_____

_____

_____

Do you have an unfinished product or idea that needs completing?

_____

_____

_____

_____

_____

_____

_____

_____

_____

_____

_____

_____

Day

8

F.O.C.U.S.

Faith and follow through
Operating by principles and not emotions
Choices are solid when facing challenges
Using good judgment when tempted to do Otherwise
Separating yourself from anything that could potentially
      Cause you to alter your course

Yesterday I talked a little about F.O.C.U.S. In today's short lesson, I want you to understand what F.O.C.U.S. means. Five areas must be understood when trying to F.O.C.U.S. Area one is **Faith** and follows through. In order to curb distractions you must have the assurance that what you are doing is necessary and is what God called you to do. Faith is the personal assurance that you heard clearly from God and you can move forward with confidence.

Area two, you must learn to **operate by principles** and not emotions. Principles according to Miriam Webster, "*is a fundamental truth, law, doctrine, or motivating force.*" Living a life of principle will lead to consistent living. Consistent living provides stability in life, which produces confidence needed to accomplish the difficult tasks in life. And with the love of God on my side, I am convinced that no matter what happens; I can stand on the assurance that the love of God supersedes any situation that could come my way.

Area three is making **solid choices** in life. When you understand how important being focused in life is you will begin to make solid choices. The time for apologies for errors and mistakes must be minimized in order to progress and move forward. The more a person matures in Christ the greater their ability to make solid life decisions. Every decision ever made in life has deeper meaning and consequences that affect you and so many other people. The greater the character the stronger the decision should be. We are a combination of the company we keep; in addition, our associations affect our thought process and what we value. If you fly with eagles, it becomes difficult to run with the chickens. Good judgment often times results from the proper associations. Iron does sharpen iron. One of the most famous sayings I heard was, "show me your friends, and I can paint a clear portrait of you." We are whom we associate with. Good judgment starts with walking closely with great people

Finally, good judgment causes me to separate myself from anyone or anything that can potentially cause me to alter my course or goals in life. This may be hard for you but I can promise failure to separate is guarantee for failure and the same results you have always received. Countless athletes year after year get in trouble because they fail to let go of what they have been delivered from. I have found that some successful people feel guilty for making it and want acceptance from those they left behind. This causes them to use bad judgment, which causes shame and disappointment to those whom they love the most. My friend, N.O.W is your time to be focused and move forward. Too many people are depending on you to reach your full potential. You have the P.O.W.E.R to make it.

Worksheet

Day

9

F.E.A.R.

Focus on losing
Excuses become common
Acknowledging defeat is regular
Reverting back to old ways and habits become a viable
option

F.E.A.R is the exact opposite of yesterday's topic of focus. F.E.A.R is a neutralizer to progression. Those that operate in fear are consistently focused on losing rather than seeing and believing for positive results. Nothing can be accomplished in life, until you have established mentally that losing is not an option. Once that resolve happens nothing becomes impossible for you.

The tower of Babel serves as a prime example of what people can do when they put their minds to accomplish something. Another example is during the 1988 Winter Olympic Games the Jamaican Bobsled team made their debut in Calgary. Those young men are prime examples of willing yourself beyond all odds. Jamaican athletes are known to be great sprinters and distance runners, not bobsledders in the Winter Olympics.

The great thing about not fearing anything is you can do whatever your heart desires as long as you do not revert back to humanity's natural instinct of under achievement. You can never acknowledge defeat in anything you do. Once defeat has been acknowledged, you might as well throw in the towel.

The greatest boxer of my time was Iron Mike Tyson; he was a fearless boxer. I loved him because he understood that nothing could stop him, but himself. His opponents feared him and when they shook his hand, you could see fear in their eyes, which was foreshadowing the beat down that was soon coming their way. However, every good thing ends at one point or another.

One fighter, James "Buster" Douglass, understood that every giant has a breaking point and you must be prepared for your opportunity. The unknown James "Buster" Douglas in February of 1990 in Tokyo, Japan understood all it took was one punch to take out the most feared boxer in the entire world. Iron Mike Tyson, did not prepare as usual and he had some personal distractions which caused him to loss his edge, and ultimately cost him the heavy weight championship of the world. After his armor was pierced, Iron Mike was never the same. Remember you are in a prize fight every day you wake up; therefore you must manage your distractions and fears, and focus on getting better each day. Remember there is power in words. God bless and have a productive day.

Worksheet

Day
10

V.O.I.C.E.S.

Verbal
Or
Implied
Communications that
Enters the
Spirit of a Person

What enters into the spirit of man is crucial to his destiny call. There are all kinds of spirits around us. Ephesians 6:12 says our fight is not against the rulers and authorities and the powers of this world's darkness, but against the spiritual powers of evil in the heavenly world. Spirits carry V.O.I.C.E.S. that will control our perception and outlook in life.

For example, James Holmes a 24-year-old former medical student did the unthinkable and went on a shooting spree that killed 12, and wounded 58 in Aurora, Colorado, as many watched the anticipated movie "The Dark Knight Rises." People just do not wake up one day and decide to become a mass murderer. Something happened inside of him, that got the attention of his spirit and his internal conscious began to tune into those sounds and V.O.I.C.E.S. in his head.

Therefore, you must be careful and monitor what you listen to and monitor those who are close enough to whisper in your ears. What we watch and choose to entertain ourselves with enters into our spirit and over the course of time we begin to eat the fruit of what has penetrated our spirit. The spirit of man is sensitive and must be protected from outside influences that have the potential to alter our destiny.

As parents, our job is to monitor our children and be guards for them. We cannot allow uncensored voices to have dominion over them anymore. Take authority over the sound waves in your life and listen to what God has to say about you. Matthew 11:15 says, "Let those with ears use them and listen (NCV)."

The Power of Words can never be underestimated. What kind of words are you hearing on a daily basis? God has special words that he wants to whisper in your ears. Today will you hear his voice? When God starts to speak, create a journal so you can remain in tune to what he is saying. As God speaks to your thoughts, you are receiving specific instructions from God the Father. Tune in and listen to what God has to say. Having and maintaining daily quiet time with God is necessary and a must for every born again believer.

Worksheet

Day
11

F.A.I.L.U.R.E.

Forgetting to learn and
Acquire the necessary
Information that
Leads to
Under achieving and low productivity while
Rationalizing and justifying in your mind why
Excellence has not been accomplished

We learn and grow from the difficult situations in life. Learning from mistakes you make is very important. Every great scientist spends years failing, seeking and searching for the answer that has perplexed the world for many years. Scientists study around the globe trying to find cures for cancer and other life ending diseases. My wife just started her battle with cancer and the technology today is much greater than it was 10 years ago. Fortunately, learning is improved over the course of time. Trial and error is the formula for greatness. My wife is beating cancer because medical science never gave up the fight against cancer.

Success is willing to take a chance while understanding that temporary failure is a necessary obstacle that brings forth victory. The Wright brothers never gave up wanting to be the first to fly. Their experimentation started in 1896 in Dayton, Ohio trying to fly their bicycle. Even though there were many failed attempts, they never gave up on the dream of flying someday. No automobile manufacturer could supply them an engine light enough to make their flight work, so they decided to design their own engine. After years of working towards that common goal on December 17, 1903, the Wright brothers took their experiment to a wind-swept beach in North Carolina. On that day, all things worked according to plan. The first flight lasted 12 seconds and covered 120 feet. The willingness of these two men changed history and the way we travel forever.

Now you can travel from North Carolina to California in 5.5 to 6 hours. It is amazing what happens when failure becomes learning for greatness. All of a sudden under-achieving is not an option, excellence becomes possible, and dreams are realized. My friend, please understand that failure is no more than a temporary setback and a learning experience that will pay tremendous dividends provided you choose not to quit. Have a great day.

Worksheet

Day

12

P.E.A.C.E.

Patiently
Embracing and
Acknowledging
Christ in
Every Situation

I have heard many great spiritual leaders talk about having peace in their lives. I have come to an understanding that having peace is not optional; it is necessary. Patience is an attitude that allows us to methodically wait on God until He answers. While waiting you must be working the plan and leave the results up to God.

P.E.A.C.E is an internal condition bathed in maturity. Once you surrender to God's omnipotence, it brings an understanding that "all things work together for his good." As Roman 8:28 clearly states for *His* good not ours. God has a plan and our job is to wait knowing that His plans, ideas and agenda will complement His design for our lives.

It amazes me that God knew us while we were yet in our mother's womb. You and I are not an accident, nor are we just the byproduct of two people being intimate. Therefore, we can and should wait patiently on Him, because he promises to give us a peace that surpasses all our understanding. As you go about your day, choose to live at peace with all men and choose peace in all situations. God bless and remember there is Power in Words.

Worksheet

Day

13

O.V.E.R.F.L.O.W.

Over abundant favor of God

Vividly seen by the World

Excellently manifested in your life that the World might understand the Power of God

Rejoicing and resting in his promises that the World might see that Power of God

Flowing in the blessings of God that the World might see the Power of God

Living above what you can personally achieve that the World might see the Power of God

Owing and giving all honor to God that the World might see the Power of God

Worshipping him in the midst of abundance that the World might see the Power of God

O.V.E.R.F.L.O.W.
Over abundant favor of God
Vividly seen by the World

We will spend the next few days talking about overflow and understanding what it means to have a biblical understanding of the word O.V.E.R.F.L.O.W. As a pastor I have learned that when preachers start talking about O.V.E.R.F.L.O.W, people start to get nervous and they begin to prepare themselves for being hit up for money from their man or woman of God. That kind of thinking has kept God's people in bondage and always waiting for a breakthrough.

I personally discovered that favor is the reward of preparation and diligence. Favor is not magic but is the result of doing the small things right in life and God will reward His people for their diligence and commitment. God never rewards laziness and lack of commitment. As Christians we are the light of the world, because of that God will allow a certain grace to be in our lives in order for people to see the power of God. Each month because of hard work and diligence, the grace of God allows me to be a top sales person month after month, and I give him all the Glory. When people ask my secret for success I pull them aside and tell them serving God with all your heart, mind and soul makes all the difference in my performance each day. Serving God is more than something I do, it is who I am.

The football season of 2012 brought much controversy as people asked did God favor Tim Tebow. The answer is yes and no. The God we serve could care less about a football game or whether Tim Tebow scores a touchdown. As I said earlier,

God could care less about sports and his real concern is how we live our lives. God is looking for people who will not be ashamed of Him and not afraid to acknowledge Him in the most public settings.

Most Christians have situational religion, they choose whether to stand or give him glory. Tim Tebow does have the favor of God because his life is representative of what a Christian should be. No, Mr. Tebow is not perfect but he is putting his money where his mouth is since he along with the Cure foundation is building a Children's Hospital in the Philippines. This is the plan of God that people are blessed so we might have the overabundant favor of God.

If you choose to allow your love for God to be vividly seen by the world you can expect an overflow in your life. Are you committed to living a life without reproach? If so, you can expect the favor of God to be vividly seen by the world. Tomorrow we will continue into an understanding on what overflow means to the body of Christ.

Worksheet

Day

14

O.V.E.R.F.L.O.W.

Excellence manifested in your life that the World might understand the Power of God

Rejoicing and resting in his promises that the World might see that Power of God

Missouri is the show me state, the same goes for every born again believer. The world wants to see our Jesus, not hear us run off the mouth and live like nothing. O.V.E.R.F.L.O.W. is needed in the life of the believer because we have to represent a Savior that is relevant and able to take care of his people. There is no greater witness than believers able to live in excellence and be an example to the world. Right now, we are facing one of the greatest economic struggles of this great country. People are hurting; the middle class is quickly becoming lower class and money is scarce. Now is the time for O.V.E.R.F.L.O.W. to take place in the lives of believer. Now is not the time to scale back.

In Genesis God used a situation similar to what we face today in the world. Joseph was in a famine, which can be compared to the present economic times we face today. God is still blessing and his people are increasing if we open our eyes and look for his glory. Our father owns the cattle upon a thousand hills; God has all we need provided we are connected to him in all we do.

For example, Liberty University represents God's light and O.V.E.R.F.L.O.W in the world today. The late Jerry Falwell had a vision for Christian Education some 40 years ago. He yielded to the call of God on his life to prepare and train young men and women for Christian discipleship all over the world. His dream is being realized as Liberty University grows by leaps and bounds. Liberty University is the largest Christian university in the World. In the midst of economic turmoil Liberty University continues to build new facilities for training and developing "Champions for Christ" I am an alumnus of Liberty University and my son is currently enrolled aspiring to be a physician while my wife pursues a Masters in Accounting.

My question to you today is will you yield to His leading that the world might see the power of God in your life? If you do, expect an O.V.E.R.F.L.O.W in your life.

Reflections from Day Eight through Fourteen

What word(s) stood out to you this week?

_____

_____

_____

_____

_____

_____

_____

_____

_____

_____

_____

Are you gaining an appreciation for words and how they must be used?

_____

_____

_____

_____

_____

_____

_____

_____

_____

_____

_____

Do you know someone that can benefit, from reading this book and why?

_____

_____

_____

_____

_____

_____

_____

_____

_____

_____

_____

Day

15

O.V.E.R.F.L.O.W.

Flowing in the blessings of God that the World might see
the Power of God
Living above what you can personally achieve that the
World might see the Power of God

When the O.V.E.R.F.L.O.W occurs, it cannot be described by words. I can remember back several years ago having my own successful business. There were so many blessing flowing my way. The only thing I regret from being so blessed was not being mature enough to handle the outpour of God's grace over my life. People often times pray for things and when the manifestation takes place, something goes wrong. We must understand it takes maturity to receive the blessing of God. Scriptures say, "I will never put on you more than you care bear

(1 Corinthians 10:13KJV)." That one applies to me. I wasted so much of God's money giving it away rather than being a good steward and trusting the leading of the Holy Spirit for guidance and direction on how to give assistance.

Many people were saved and considered trusting God because of the testimony that Nicole and I shared. We did live above what we personally thought was achievable. God blessed our lives so much the first few years we were married. As I look back now I understand, what God was doing in my life? He was preparing both Nicole and me for more. The overflow is never completely for you; it is a tool to bring people closer to Jesus. It is an opportunity to point people to the goodness of God.

Get a mind for more and start thinking with an overflow mentality. Do not just settle for the way things have always been. You are engineered and designed for more. When was the last time you stirred up those gifts from within? You were created to do more. There are people waiting to benefit from the ideas, skills and ability God has given you. Are you getting it now? Tomorrow, we will conclude on the. O.V.E.R.F.L.O.W

Worksheet

Day

16

O.V.E.R.F.L.O.W.

Owing and giving all honor to God that the World might
   see the Power of God
Worshipping him in the midst of abundance that the
   World might see that God provides for His people

In order for O.V.E.R.F.L.O.W to be sustained there must be a level of humility and realization that God did it all for you. I have found that people have a short memory when it comes to honoring God when he provides or honoring the people God uses to provide. As a pastor countless times, I have seen our church pray that God would bless certain individuals with sufficient transportation, jobs, or shelter. It almost never fails after the blessing comes, departure from church shortly happens. That rather bothered me for a while until God spoke these words in my spirit: "no matter how things look on the outside I have ultimate control of each situation."

Therefore worshipping God in the midst of abundance can be hard for many believers because of the voices they hear or have heard in the past. Abundance is great when the mind has been prepared for increase. Increase is a great thing when you understand the pressure and frustration that comes with the blessing. Countless people have won the lottery and within a short amount of time, all the fortune is lost. God will never put on his people more than they are able to handle. The best way to prepare for increase is to stretch your mental borders and you will soon find yourself shifting from lack to O.V.E.R.F.L.O.W. What you want in life must be written down and it is amazing how things begin to fall in place once you take action to bring it to past. Seeing is believing.

Worksheet

Day

17

F.R.U.S.T.R.A.T.I.O.N.

Failure to measure up to initial expectation

Running into bricks walls

Unexpected delays

Shortage of the necessary resources to meet immediate needs

Temptation to quit and walk away

Ready to throw in the towel and try something else

Anxiety kicks in because you are sick and tired of being sick and tired

Time seems to be running out along with your patience to endure

Information over Load

Out of Options

Nothing seems to go right

F.R.U.S.T.R.A.T.I.O.N.
Failure to measure up to initial expectation
Running into bricks walls

Most of America is feeling a certain level of F.R.U.S.T.R.A.T.I.O.N. Frustration often brings with it many levels of emotions that very seldom help the problem at hand. These tough economic times are causing people to point fingers and play the blame game. Republicans are blaming Democrats, Democrats are blaming Republicans, and the Independents just want someone to pay them some attention. The truth be told we have a little part in what is happening today; greed caused us to mortgage away our future.

There was no way one presidential term could clean up the mess that started decades ago. We must understand that what goes up must come down at some point. Yet, the down is never so bad when you prepare. Because of the days America failed to prepare, we are left pointing fingers with no real answer in sight. God is the only one that can solve these terrible economic times.

Planning is the key to minimizing brick walls in your life. F.R.U.S.T.R.A.T.I.O.N is manageable once the cycle is broken and new strategies are put in place. Do not allow your frustration to dominate the majority of your day; do something to counter what has taken a turn for the worse. Remember brick walls are designed to come down one brick at a time. Do not allow those brick walls of F.R.U.S.T.R.A.T.I.O.N. to take your joy and steal your productivity. Tomorrow we will continue learning how to manage F.R.U.S.T.R.A.T.I.O.N and continue on the path to living a maximized life that pleases God.

Worksheet

Day

18

F.R.U.S.T.R.A.T.I.O.N.

Unexpected Delays

Nothing causes more F.R.U.S.T.R.A.T.I.O.N than being delayed. In the natural, being held up seems like a waste of time. Our society is fast pace. Things are changing all the time and we have very little to no conversation or interaction with people anymore. Families are no longer sitting down together and eating supper together. Everyone seems to be in a rush. There is after school sports and practice and both parents now have to work to make ends meet. We are always striving for finding the latest and the next greatest technology.

Apple has trained a new generation of technology buffs; they are always searching for the next new gadget. My son just got a new I Phone 4s with 16 gigs and some other things I never used or even understand. Have you ever considered that some delays are good? We need time to be still. God wants all of us and we have become so busy that he gets 45 minutes on Sunday, if we do not have other things to do.

In the spiritual realm often times God will slow down his people in order to get their attention. My friends, if you are a person that has so many things to do that you do not have time to think, then you are too busy. We must slow down, understand, and enjoy life. No matter what you do in life, nothing lives longer than time. Today sit down and let your body rest for a few minutes. You will find that life has more meaning when you find time to reflect, think, and meditate. Do not let F.R.U.S.T.R.A.T.I.O.N. rob you of peace. Do the best you can and leave the rest up to God.

Worksheet

Day

19

F.R.U.S.T.R.A.T.I.O.N.

Shortage of the necessary resources to meet immediate
    needs
Temptation to quit and walk away
Ready to throw in the towel and try something else

Every person at one time or another has experienced a shortage
of the necessary resources to meet immediate needs. The one
shortage that most people experience is the lack of funds to meet
ongoing financial obligations. I can remember back several years
ago when my business closed, it was as if I was watching my life
pass me by in slow motion. It seemed so surreal I never thought it
would happen to me. "Life flipped on me" as my pastor, Bishop
Rosie S. O'Neal would often say. When life flips on you the only
thing you can do is hold on, take a deep breath, and keep trying

until something sticks. Most people fall into depression and even become suicidal. I was that person. Life had flipped on me and I was frustrated and not equipped to do anything about it.

I was tempted to walk away from all my obligations and commit suicide. I started thinking if I kill myself my wife would have enough money to live happily ever after. How stupid was that. Satan was planting seeds in my mind to do the unthinkable. After a while, "I came to myself" just like the prodigal son. I began to understand that no temptation that I faced was uncommon to man (1 Cor. 10:13). God confirmed in my spirit that He never left me, but He wanted to use this experience to teach me to fight and believe in Him as provider. God is our provider and we must not be caught up in worshipping things and forget to worship the provider of all things.

After that brief moment of insanity, I understood that throwing in the towel was not an option. God challenged me to start over and learn to trust Him, and to live each day as if it was my last. Managing F.R.U.S.T.R.A.T.I.O.N. is part of the learning process. Those that are over comers are continuously learning how to adapt, overcome, and conquer adverse situations. Remember you can control your emotions rather than your emotions controlling you. F.R.U.S.T.R.A.T.I.O.N is a manageable emotion.

Worksheet

Day

20

F.R.U.S.T.R.A.T.I.O.N.

Anxiety kicks in because you are sick and tired of being
sick and tired

*"Be anxious for nothing, but in everything by prayer and
supplication, with thanksgiving, let your requests be made known
to God; ⁷ and the peace of God, which surpasses all understanding,
will guard your hearts and minds through Christ Jesus."*

Phil. 4:6-7

F.R.U.S.T.R.A.T.I.O.N. causes a high level of anxiety to
take place. It does not matter whether you are saved or lost
everyone gets frustrated and anxiety kicks in. God wants to give
his people peace in the midst of the storm. Jesus was sleeping
peacefully on the boat when his disciples encountered a small

storm and they went to pieces. Many times as Christians, the minute things begin to fall apart we forget to praise him for his faithfulness in past situations.

Several months ago, my wife was diagnosed with stage 2 breast cancer. I felt an overwhelming anxiety like never before. I could not show any signs of worry because she was depending on me for strength. My congregation looked to me for strength. My family looked to me for strength. Then I realized I was not able to be strong enough for all those people. My heavenly father told me to cast all my cares and concerns on Him, and leave the results up to Him and that is exactly what I did.

That Sunday morning during praise and worship, I fell to my knees and worshipped him for at least 30 minutes; I held up the church service. After getting the release I needed, it felt like the world had been lifted off my shoulders. I soon discovered I was carrying a burden that was never meant for me to carry. From that moment, forward God gave me a peace that surpassed my understanding. Together with the help of God, the cancer is defeated and we are just waiting for the final report of good news.

Anxiety is an emotion that can be managed and if not handled properly it will take control of your life. By nature I am passive aggressive in personality, but God has taught me through my trials to get control of anxiety and deal with the situation upfront. Whenever you let things fester, it becomes larger and harder to deal with over the course of time.

Worksheet

Day
21

F.R.U.S.T.R.A.T.IO.N.

Time seems to be running out along with your patience
    to endure
Information over Load
Out of Options
Nothing seems to go right

Today's lesson will conclude my teachings on F.R.U.S.T.R.A.T.I.O.N. I just wanted to make sure you had a clear understanding of F.R.U.S.T.R.A.T.I.O.N. and how to manage those emotions. When things are not going right and it appears as if time is running out, do not quit. Life has a way of flipping on you and you must understand that you are never out of options.

God has a way of providing for his people in unconventional ways. Moses and the children of Israel's journey is the perfect example of not quitting in the midst of frustration. God took care of his people and provided for all their needs during their 40 year journey of disobedience. How much more will our heavenly father take care of his people, who walk upright and live in obedience to Him.

F.R.U.S.T.R.A.T.I.O.N. is an emotion that causes one to feel hopeless and doomed if something doesn't happen soon. God wants to use those emotions to teach His people total dependence on him. As I look back at my life, God has taught me tremendous lessons through my points of frustration. As I look back those moments of frustrations were wasted energy and could have been used in other positive ways.

Reverend Eric Miles made a statement to me several years ago, that continues to ring in my ear at the moment F.R.U.S.T.R.A.T.I.O.N. wants to permeate my thinking. He stated "duties never conflict." What he said was so profound, "God knows I am a husband, God knows I am a father, God knows I am a pastor, and God knows I work a full time job other than ministry" and suddenly it hit me. Why am I stressing? God has everything in control and my responsibility is to be faithful in each situation and leave the results and timing of things up to God. Since hearing those words God has given me a peace that passes all understanding and he will do the same for you provided you choose not to be frustrated. Remember there is Power in Words.

Reflections from day fifteen through twenty

What is your greatest frustration or challenge and how you plan to fix it using the "Power of Words?"

_____

_____

_____

_____

_____

_____

_____

_____

_____

_____

_____

_____

_____

_____

_____

_____

_____

_____

_____

_____

_____

_____

_____

_____

R.I.S.K.

Reasonable assurance that something different must
   transpire
It is necessary to step in unchartered waters for change
Separating yourself from those who only talk about
   change
Keep striving for more until the manifestation appears

R.I.S.K.

Reasonable assurance that something different must transpire
   It is necessary to step in unchartered waters for change

Those that are willing to take R.I.S.K. position themselves
to receiving a higher reward than those that only murmur
and complain about their situations. R.I.S.K. is the reasonable

assurance that something different must transpire in your life. In life, nothing is guaranteed therefore you must never be afraid to make the necessary changes. Insanity is clearly doing the same things day after day and year after year expecting different results.

Life is what we make it. Do not be a person who knows what to do but is unwilling to progress to make things happen. Walking in unchartered waters bring excitement and intrigue to life. Just think; every business venture was initially unchartered waters with little to no guarantee for success.

Chick-fil-A walked in unchartered waters as they made a decision to never open on Sundays. Many restaurants critics said that business model would never work. Chick-fil-A started the family oriented business model in 1965 and within two years in business, they decided to stop selling burgers and refine their menu to chicken only. Today Chic-fil-A surpassed burger giant McDonalds averaging 2.7 million dollars in sales per store. Taking the proper R.I.S.K. following by conviction will often produce dividends provided you don't quit along the way.

Worksheet

Day

23

R.I.S.K.

Separating yourself from those who only talk about
   change
Keep striving for more until the manifestation appears

When you take *R.I.S.K.* in life, you become part of an elite class of people. Elite in the since you are willing to do what is necessary to achieve what your heart desires. Separating yourself from pretenders in life makes all the difference. As parents, we chose to pull our son out of public school and put him into an environment that focused on Christian principles and God's standard for living. It was a hard decision pulling him from his natural environment to a place that had stricter guidelines, policies, and procedures.

Now looking back it was the best decision and sacrifice we could have made as parents. I cannot give the school all the credit. As parents, we raised him to love God and respect people and the school just supported what we taught at home. Now he is a productive well-rounded young man who can adapt to almost any situation and can fit in with almost any group of people. When you decide to step outside your common element, you become well rounded, able to understand different cultures and people. Are you willing to separate from those who hold you back from being all God called you to be?

Finally, when you separate it causes you to strive for more in life. There is nothing wrong with wanting to be more and do more in life. I must warn you, if you fail to separate, it will hinder your ability to strive for more and it is unlikely that manifestation will ever take place. My greatest fear in life is being an old man someday talking about what could have happened if I had taken the necessary *R.I.S.K.* in life. I cannot bear the fact of not accomplishing the goals I set out to do in life. I firmly believe God created us as individuals to contribute in life. We should be living life on the edge and if we are not we are simply taking up too much space. My friend, do an assessment of your life. Are you trying to live life without taking *a R.I.S.K.*? If so, you will never accomplish those dreams and ambitions that you so eagerly wait to explore. You can do it, I am doing it, and you can too.

Worksheet

Day

24

R.E.W.A.R.D.S.

Repay for
Embracing challenges and
Working hard
Accepting nothing short of victory
Receiving due compensation for
Doing what your heart desired for
Stepping outside the box

R.E.W.A.R.D.S.
Repay for
Excepting challenges and
Working hard

Yesterday's devotions thoroughly talked about taking calculated risks. *R.I.S.K.* and R.E.W.A.R.D.S. go hand and hand. Those that reap the greatest R.E.W.A.R.D.S. in life are risk takers. R.E.W.A.R.D.S. is repayment for risks that have been taken in life. The 2012 Summer Olympics in London is probably the best example of rewards for taking risks. An Olympic athlete trains for years on end for an opportunity to compete against the world's best every four years. The ultimate reward is a gold medal for being the best in the world in your sport. Even though a silver medal reflects you are second best in the world, no one competes for the opportunity to be second best, and everyone wants to win the gold.

What separates the gold medal winner from the silver medal winner sometimes is 1/100 of a second. The small span of time is the difference between major endorsements and being an after thought. No one remembers the person that came in second only those who had the ability to close the deal. Nothing beats hard work and commitment to your craft. Whatever your job, profession or desire remember to work hard and expect the proper pay for your sacrifice.

Worksheet

Day

25

R.E.W.A.R.D.S.

Accepting nothing short of victory
Receiving due compensation for
Doing what your heart desired and
Stepping outside the box

People that are driven will not accept anything short of victory. Victorious living must become your mindset as you strive towards receiving your due compensation for the work you do in life.

Several years ago as a young business professional, an older man once shared an amazing fact with me that have made all the difference in my life regarding R.E.W.A.R.D.S. and fair compensation for the work I do. The wise old man stated, "Son, no one can truly ever pay you what you are worth." When I first heard that statement, I thought the older person was crazy. As I have matured in life, I found that statement to be very true. What I realized later in life is sometimes it takes people a while to understand the value that you personally bring to situations.

Some of the greatest people in America often times do large jobs with little to no compensation. For example, the countless people in America that run homeless shelters, substance abuse centers and other social and civic programs are great examples of jobs with a lot of responsibility and little compensation. Also in many of the churches all across America, countless volunteers spend long hours helping their ministries to grow and be a blessing to many people.

I am amazed at the pride of those individuals that are doing their jobs in excellence. I have learned that the greatest R.E.W.A.R.D.S for many people is just someone telling them thank you for a job well done. I am amazed how far a thank you will go in life. Those that are successful in life have learned how to make people feel good in what they do well. When was the last time you told someone thank you for a job well done. You will be amazed at the response you will get from those that assist you in life. Have a great day and remember to reward those that help make your life better.

Worksheet

Day
26

F.A.V.O.R.

Faith for what you do not have
Accelerated into what was closed off
Victory in what should have defeated you
Obstacles removed that once hindered
Right timing from God from what could have been lost
     or never realized

The F.A.V.O.R. of God is awesome. F.A.V.O.R. is showing exceptional kindness towards an individual. The context in which I will use F.A.V.O.R. is God's kindness towards those whom He loves. Yes, we serve a kind and awesome God, but He does require something from His people in order to see manifestations of Favor. There is a lifestyle of faith and clean living that must be expressed in the life of a believer before F.A.V.O.R. can work. 2 Kings 4:1-4 exemplifies this:

"Now there cried a certain woman of the wives of the sons of the prophets unto Elisha, saying, Thy servant my husband is dead; and thou knowest that thy servant did fear the Lord: and the creditor is come to take unto him my two sons to be bondmen.

And Elisha said unto her, What shall I do for thee? Tell me, what hast thou in the house? And she said, Thine handmaid hath not anything in the house, save a pot of oil. Then he said, Go, borrow thee vessels abroad of all thy neighbours, even empty vessels; borrow not a few.

And when thou art come in, thou shalt shut the door upon thee and upon thy sons, and shalt pour into all those vessels, and thou shalt set aside that which is full."

God met the widow's needs through her own obedience. The F.A.V.O.R. of God is accessed through our ability to follow instructions. We must understand having the F.A.V.O.R. of God is not magic, but consistent faithful obedient living accesses the F.A.V.O.R. of God in our lives. God wants to supply all our needs but we must be willing to follow through on what he requires from us. Upon doing that, my friend, you will access and experience the F.A.V.O.R. of God like never before. The widow had all her needs met through borrowing vessels as God had instructed her. The oiled poured as she had vessels to pour into. We must give God something to pour into. What are your dreams, desires, and ambitions? Will you be obedient today and let him pour into your life. God bless you and remember the F.A.V.O.R. of God waits on your obedience.

Worksheet

Day
27

R.A.C.E.

Running with the invention of winning
Always acknowledging the strength of God while
Carefully
Embracing the grace to Finish Strong

As a former athlete, I was trained to have a winner's mindset. I understand some say winning or losing is not important, but it is how you play the game. That saying is so far from the truth. Not only is winning important winning is the only thing. While maintaining the winner's mentality you cannot lose yourself in pursuit of the prize. While striving for victory you must keep your core values in place, which allows you to maintain balance and consistency in life. The person who came up with that phrase definitely was not an athlete because no one trains to compete with the intention of losing.

Life has a way of throwing curve balls and you must be prepared to deal with them. Often times those curve balls can cause you to withdraw from certain situations in life. No one plans for sickness and disease; sometimes health issues arise, and you have to deal with the matter at hand. Even when those times arise, life is still going on and you must mentally adjust in order to get back into the race of life. Sometimes there are employment gaps when you lose a job, which is just another delay in the R.A.C.E. You must gather yourself and come up with a different game plan.

Are you starting to realize that everything in life is a R.A.C.E. and you must be prepared for minor and major changes along the way? Therefore, anything that I can personally control, I have no choice but to have the intentions of winning. Winning has a way of becoming contagious to those who are close to you. In order to remain balanced and humble in the pursuit of victory there must always be a focus on God and His strength and grace to finish the race.

Life is one big R.A.C.E. that we compete against everyday. The greatest race that we all face is the race against time. No man can beat Father Time but a conscious mindset must be developed to maximize every second of the day to finish strong. As you approach day 31 understand that you must learn to pace yourself and commit to running with strength, courage, and integrity. You can never win believing that you will lose. The R.A.C.E. is yours to win understanding that you are built for the storms of life.

Worksheet

Day
28

P.A.I.N.

Physical and mental discomfort which produces
Anguish and
Intense feelings of misery, sufferings and
Never ending grief that can only be cured by God

I have experienced many kinds of P.A.I.N. in my life. Just recently, I have watched my wife battle breast cancer. I would give anything to take the P.A.I.N. away from her. The discomfort experienced on a weekly basis is very intense. I am so very proud of her; she has a champion heart and mind. In the midst of her situation, she finds O.P.P.O.R.T.U.N.I.T.Y to encourage people all around her.

During her chemo treatment, she searches the room to find some one who may be depressed or struggling with the treatment. The woman I married 17 years ago was a shy very, reserved person. Over the past years, God has done a tremendous job creating what He desired her to be. I am amazed at the omnipotence and omniscience of God.

God has a plan for our lives. I truly believe that many people will get to know Christ through Nicole's determination to beat cancer. We have claimed victory already. After 5 weeks, the tumor cannot be traced by human hands. God uses medicine and faith to heal His people and according to Isaiah 53:5 *"we are healed because or his wounds."*

P.A.I.N. has a way of teaching us to be strong. The pain of losing a loved one should teach us to appreciate every moment we have with the ones we love the most. Romans 8:28-29 says, *"We know that in everything God works for the good of those who love him. They are the people he called, because that was his plan (NCV)."*

Worksheet

W.I.N.N.E.R.S.

Workers of
Intensity
Never taking anything for granted
Never assuming victory will come without
Extra practice and a dedicated
Regiment that
Separates them from amateurs

Gabby Douglas is a household name because she decided to do something about her future. W.I.N.N.E.R.S. understand the multitude of sacrifices and commitment it takes to be great in life. At the tender age of 14, she along with her mother decided that she needed better training in order to obtain the gold at the 2012 Summer Olympics. The training she needed to become great was in Iowa, half way across the United States.

I cannot even begin comprehending the courage it took for her to leave home and stay with strangers for two years. Gabby had what it took to be great. W.I.N.N.E.R.S. are wired differently; they are focused and committed to the regiment knowing that sacrifice is part of the process. Because she had a commitment to win, Gabby Douglas is the first woman of color and African American Gymnast in Olympic history to win a gold medal. Also, she is the first American gymnast to win gold in both the individual all-around and team competitions at the same Olympics.

Finally, W.I.N.N.E.R.S. are not afraid to separate from whatever prevents them from moving forward in life. Seperating from the pact is necessary in many causes. W.I.N.N.E.R.S. understand wasted energy and effort is the primary ingredient to F.A.I.L.U.R.E. One millisecond is the difference between winning the gold or silver. You do not have time to waste. Internalize your goals and let nothing hold you back.

Worksheet

Day
30

V.I.C.T.O.R.Y.

Valuing All Lessons Learned
Ignoring All Desire to Quit
Conquering All Fear of Losing
Testing and Pushing beyond Comfort
Open to Change
Ready to Start
Yielding to Nothing but Excellence

When this 31-day journey was written, I had you in mind. This book for some will be that this is the first book they have read from beginning to end. That is a V.I.C.T.O.R.Y. moment for you in itself. V.I.C.T.O.R.Y. in life is the result of doing small things successfully over the course of time. Through research, I discovered that doing the same thing over a 31-day time period becomes a habit and habits become a lifestyle. True V.I.C.T.O.R.Y. in life is valuing and internalizing each lesson, you have learned. No matter who you are, there is a lesson to be learned from any situation.

Victorious others often times ignore the urge to quit; quitting becomes habitual if done on a regular basis. In addition when you choose not to quit, conquering fears become more manageable. There is one fear I have not conquered yet and that is eating a tomato; somehow, that one vegetable intimidates my stomach. My son laughs as I take the tomato off a sandwich that has been ordered at a restaurant.

V.I.C.T.O.R.Y. will always test and push you beyond the point of comfort. Being a former football player, I trained year round to become bigger, stronger, and faster. Never was it easy to push my body beyond normal, but the results paid off each season. Pushing provided results, and at the tender weight of 225 pounds I was able to bench press over 520 pounds, about 2.5 times my body weight. That V.I.C.T.O.R.Y. was the result of years of training and personally committing to becoming great. That commitment caused me to be ranked 17th in the U.S. in my weight class among those competing in power lifting. I will always be grateful for the experience in competing among the best in the country.

My friend, you are competing every day for, V.I.C.T.O.R.Y. Understand that your greatest competition and challenge in life is the person you see in the mirror every day. In order to achieve your life goals and win you must always remain open to change, and never accept anything from yourself other than your very best. V.I.C.T.O.R.Y. is possible provided you know and understand there is Power in Words. What words are you declaring today to make your life different? Remember the V.O.I.C.E. you hear the most is yours. God bless you and remember there is Power in Words.

Worksheet

Day
31

THE FLOW OF WORDS

Today is the combination of all the Words we have discovered over the past 30 days. I guarantee if you used the words on a regular basis your vocabulary will change and you perspective on life will be better.

W.O.R.D.S give you the **O.P.P.O.R.T.U.N.I.T.Y.** to get **P.O.W.E.R.** and they permit your **D.R.E.A.M.S.** to come true that forces your real **P.O.T.E.N.T.I.A.L.** to be unleashed **N.O.W.**, which causes an individual to live a better life immediately. Therefore **E.N.R.I.C.H.** your mind and **F.O.C.U.S.** on the impossible without allowing **F.E.A.R.** to dominate your thought process. Please understand wrong **V.O.I.C.E.S.** will promote **F.A.I.L.U.R.E.** and you will not live in **P.E.A.C.E.**, which slows down your **O.V.E.R.F.L.O.W.** that leads to

F.R.U.S.T.R.A.T.I.O.N. A change is necessary therefore; you must be willing to take calculated **R.I.S.K.** to receive your due **R.E.W.A.R.D.S.** The **F.A.V.O.R.** of God awaits a person that fights through the temptation and continues the **R.A.C.E.** regardless of the **P.A.I.N.** because **W.I.N.N.E.R.S.** are determined to let nothing hold them back from **V.I.C.T.O.R.Y.** Congratulations my friend! You have made it through the 31st day journey of words; do you feel The Power of Words?

Congratulations you finished the book, now the real work begins. Follow these simple instructions for becoming the person you always wanted to be. You hold the power for change and increase. Your associations and accountability has great influence on how consistent you become. Change is hard work and requires effort.

- Find a person(s) that you love and trust the most share those thoughts you wrote down previously and ask them to hold you accountable.
- Also suggest, that your friend get their own book and complete the 31 day journey themselves, which will allow them to feel your experience.
- Each make an effort to enhance your vocabulary and your thought patterns, "Words Have Power" please understand, you get back what you release into the atmosphere.
- Review this daily journal of "Words" once a month to remind yourself, how far you have come and where you are going.
- Finally, send me an email to receive a free inspirational word of the week; I can be reached at amvandyke@ thepowerofwordsbook.com

ABOUT THE AUTHOR

The best words to describe my personality is honest, transparent and sincere, I was born in a small town called Smithfield, Virginia better known as the "Ham" capital of the world. Growing up in a small town I always dreamed of doing something special with my life. The small town atmosphere taught me how to get along with people and to see the good in everyone. One of my teachers once told me, with a name like Anthony Monroe VanDyke, you are bound to do great things. I never forgot those words; she prophetically spoken into my life.

Sports was my claim to fame in high school, I played football, ran track and lifted weights. Like many young men I dreamed of playing professional football and coming back home to be an elementary school teacher and a football coach. The destiny track began to take form at Chowan College a two-year university in Murfreesboro, North Carolina. While attending that small college, I learned many life skills. The highlight of my tenure at Chowan College was playing inside linebacker on the football team. My on the field success opened the door for me to become team captain and to be voted Most Valuable Player by my peers. Looking back Chowan College taught me leadership skills that I am still using today. Upon graduation I attended Liberty University to finish my college education, at Liberty University life took a turn. I was hurt the first week of football practice. God got hold of my heart and called me into full time ministry by my second semester. The big picture began to unfold at Liberty University. The late Revered Jerry Falwell taught us to become visionaries and our personal responsibility to impact the world in a positive manner.

The training I received at Liberty University prepared me for the next chapter in my life. The next chapter of my life included getting married to my wife Nicole; she has been a rock in my life over the past 20 years. We have an awesome son name Nick who attends Liberty University. Nicole and I remain partners in everything thing I do. She is a successful accountant and corporate manager. We started New Community Christian Center Church, a ministry centered on changing and impacting the lives of people. Thousands have been and continue to be impacted by our ministry each and every day. *The Power of Words* represents the first step of sharing our gifts with the world.

The Success and Accomplishments:

- Husband of One Wife (Nicole)
- Father of one son (Nick)

- Former World Class Power Lifter, Benched Pressed Over 500 pounds
- Lectured Students in Public Schools Across America
- Founding Pastor of New Community Christian Center
- Public Speaker
- Former Real Estate Investor
- Former Owner and Founder of ABC Mortgage Funding (Suffolk)
- Teacher and Mentor to Multiple Real Estate Investors
- Job Counselor and Career Advisor to many
- Recognized as Top Sales person for Chrysler Automotive Corporation in 2012

Printed in the USA
CPSIA information can be obtained
at www.ICGtesting.com
JSHW021936160424
61205JS00004BA/341

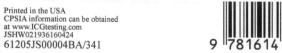